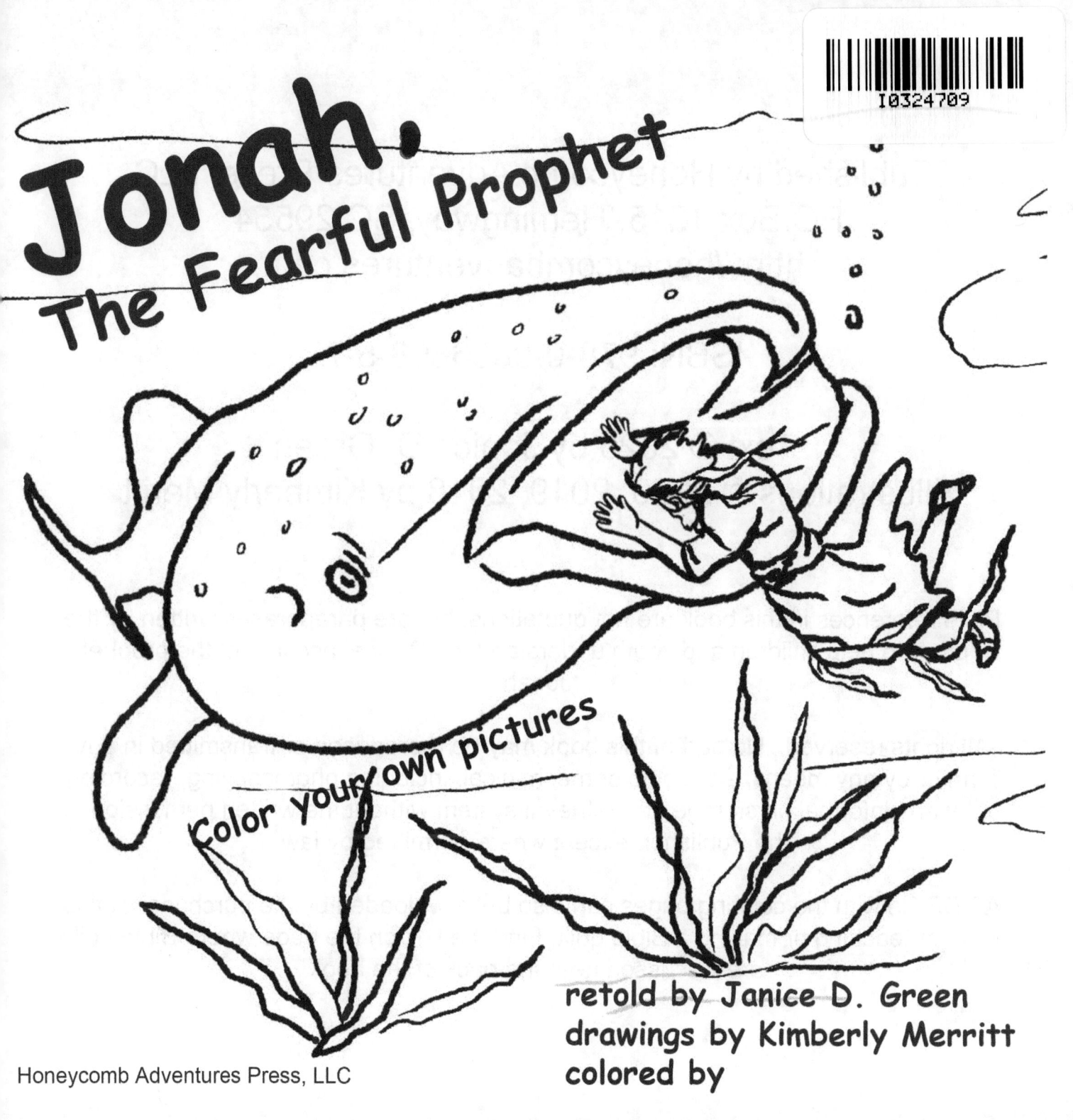

Published by Honeycomb Adventures Press, LLC
PO Box 1215, Hemingway, SC 29554.
http://honeycombadventures.com

ISBN: 978-0-9836808-5-7

Text © 2020 by Janice D. Green
Illustrations © 2020, 2019, 2018 by Kimberly Meritt

Bible references in this book are not quotations, but are paraphrases written by the author to help children and youth understand the Biblical account of the prophet Jonah.

All rights reserved. No part of this book may be reproduced or transmitted in any form or by any means, electronic or mechanical, including photocopying, recording or by any information storage and retrieval system without the written permission of the Publisher, except where permitted by law.

A PDF file with the coloring pages can also be downloaded by the purchaser of this book for teaching or making a Bible quilt. Find the link on the page where Bible quilts are discussed near the back of the book.

God told Jonah to go to Nineveh and tell the people he was going to destroy their city. But Jonah did not want to go. He was afraid of the people who lived in Nineveh.

Jonah had heard many terrible things about the people of Nineveh. He wanted God to destroy those horrible people and their city.

Jonah pouted. What if the people listened to him? What if they stopped doing wicked things? And what if God saw and changed his mind?

So Jonah made up his mind to go in the opposite direction. He went to the harbor and got on a ship to sail to a place called Tarshish—far away from Nineveh.

God watched Jonah go on that ship, so he sent a storm with fierce winds and crashing waves to toss the ship around on the sea.

The frightened sailors wanted to make the ship lighter so it would not sink. They threw their heavy crates and boxes into the sea.

The sailors cried out to their false gods. But the storm raged on becoming wilder than before.

All this time Jonah slept in his bunk below the deck. The ship's captain found Jonah and shouted, "How can you sleep in this storm? Get up and pray to your god!"

"Somebody did something terrible or this wouldn't be happening," the sailors said. So the sailors cast lots to see who was responsible for the storm. Casting lots in those days was like when we toss dice or draw straws to decide something. The lots pointed to Jonah.

"Are you the reason this storm came up?" they screamed at Jonah. "Where are you from? Who is your god?"

Jonah knew the sailors were right. He knew he tried to run away from God.

"I am a Hebrew," Jonah said, "and I worship the God of heaven who created the land and sea. Pick me up and throw me into the sea and the storm will stop. This storm is my fault. "

The sailors were afraid to throw Jonah into the sea. They tried to row back to shore, but the waves rose higher and tossed them about so they couldn't row.

The sailors prayed to Jonah's God. They begged him not to be angry with them for what they had to do. Then they threw Jonah over the side of the ship.

Immediately, the wind died down, and the sea became peaceful.

The amazed sailors eyes grew wide and they feared Jonah's God even more. They offered a sacrifice to God and made promises to him.

Jonah closed his eyes and held his breath as he sank beneath the waves.

He drifted into a deep valley between underwater mountains. Jonah felt seaweed wrap around his head.

Jonah had run away from God, and now he was tangled in seaweed at the bottom of the sea. Was he going to die? Would he ever see God's holy temple again?

But God did not let Jonah die. He still had a job for Jonah to do.

The same God who created the sea and everything in it made a huge fish – it might have been a whale – and sent it to swallow Jonah.

The big fish kept Jonah captive in its belly for three days and nights.

Jonah could feel his hands and face and knew he was still alive.

"You heard my prayer from the bottom of the sea!" Jonah said. "You rescued me from the storm and the waves. I'm still alive!"

"I thought of you when I felt the seaweed wrap around my head at the bottom of the sea. I was almost dead," Jonah said to God, "and I prayed that I could again offer sacrifices and keep all my promises to you."

Jonah's heart burst with praise for God. Even though he was still in the big fish, he had faith in God. He knew God sent the fish to save him.

God heard Jonah's prayer. He ordered the great fish to spit Jonah out onto the land.

Jonah looked up at the blue sky. He saw birds and grass and trees, and he was happy to be alive.

God said to Jonah, "Get up, go to Nineveh, and give my message to the people."

This time Jonah obeyed God.

Jonah hurried to Nineveh. Over and over he shouted to the people, "The city of Nineveh will be destroyed in forty days!"

Jonah was faithful to his promise. Nineveh was a huge city. It took Jonah three long, hard days to walk down all those streets, and God protected him every step of the way.

He shouted his message everywhere he went. "God said the city of Nineveh will be destroyed in forty days!"

Jonah did not stop until everyone heard the message.

The people of Nineveh believed Jonah. They stopped eating. They took off their comfortable clothes and put on rough, scratchy sackcloth to show God how sorry they felt.

Even the king changed to scratchy sackcloth. He plopped down in dust and ashes and made a new rule.

"Everyone must stop being wicked," he said. "Everybody, even the animals, must wear sackcloth. And people and animals must stop eating and drinking. Everyone must pray to God."

The king hoped God would hear their prayers, change his mind, and not destroy their city.

God saw the people stop eating.

He saw them put on scratchy sackcloth.

He heard their prayers.

And he saw them stop doing the bad things they had been doing.

So God had mercy on the people of Nineveh. He did not destroy their city.

But Jonah pouted. Anger boiled inside him—at God. He still did not like Nineveh. He did not want God to show them mercy.

God had another lesson for Jonah. God caused a vine to grow quickly, and it gave Jonah a shady place to rest. Jonah liked the vine.

The next day God sent a worm to eat through the vine so it dried up and died. When the vine died Jonah said, "I'm so angry! I want to die."

God said to Jonah, "You did nothing to make the vine grow. You should not care when it died. I care about the people and children in Nineveh. They are more important than this vine."

The Bible doesn't tell us if Jonah's heart softened. But we know God was patient with Jonah.

Questions to think about

Have you ever done the opposite from what you were told to do? What happened?

Whose lives were in danger when Jonah disobeyed God? Did you ever do something wrong that caused other people to get hurt?

What did the sailors learn about God?

What do you think it would feel like inside a big fish or whale? What would it smell like?

Have you ever been in so much trouble you thought you would never get through it? What happened? Did you remember to pray to God about your problem? Do you have any problems you think are too big for God to handle?

How do you think Jonah felt when he was alive and back on the land? Can you remember a time when God answered a prayer for you? How did you feel?

Wearing sackcloth and sitting in dust and ashes was the way people in Bible times showed they were very sad or sorry for what they had done. What are some things you might do today to show you are truly sorry for something you did?

Have you seen something good happen to a person who had done mean things? How did you feel? How did God say Jonah should feel after God forgave the mean people of Nineveh?

Jonah wasn't a perfect prophet. But God gave him a second chance. When have you had a second chance to get something right?

Jonah

Across
3. What did Jonah do when he was in the belly of the fish? (He _____)
6. What did Jonah get on to go to Tarshish?
7. Where did God tell Jonah to go?
9. What did Jonah tell the people God was going to do to Nineveh?
10. What did God give Jonah one day and then let it die the next?
11. What did the people of Nineveh wear to show they were sorry?

Down
1. What happened when the ship sailed out to sea?
2. What wrapped around Jonah's head at the bottom of the sea?
4. What did God send to rescue Jonah from the bottom of the sea?
5. Where did Jonah decide to go instead of Nineveh?
8. Who did the sailors blame for causing the storm?

Across: 3 Prayed, 6 Ship, 7 Nineveh, 9 Destroy, 10 Vine, 11 Sackcloth. Down: 1 Storm, 2 Seaweed, 4 Fish, 5 Tarshish, 8 Jonah.

Jonah Word Search

ASHES
CARGO
CAST LOTS
DESTROY
FAST
JONAH
KING
MERCY
NINEVEH
OVERBOARD
PRAISE
PRAY
SACKCLOTH
SHIP
TARSHISH
VINE
WICKED
WORM

```
D R V N B J W M E K I N G J S
E I W I I Q O S R J W C X T Z
S M E R C Y I N D C M Z O D F
T K R G T A L R A N I L L N L
R E O Q R A A Z A H T Q X N M
O B M P H O R S H S Y E M R R
Y A M K B S M S A J T T O F C
A U D R W A N C H S G W N V B
H C E F T C L I A I U X A I K
D V M Y S K N F N A S R A N W
O G A E S C C B K E F H T E I
Y R H S V L F A K M V A R J C
P S E H X O W X R F G E F L K
A U Q I E T Z O S G E C H E E
K G D P P H S Z J X O Z V P D
```

Bible Quilt – A Family Activity

A fun way to share your excitement about Bible stories with your child is to create a Bible quilt. Imagine a quilt covering your child's bed with pictures of Bible stories. Can you visualize the child pointing to one picture and then another asking to hear the stories again? This is the vision for the Bible Quilts at www.BibleQuilts.com, a sister blog to Honeycomb Adventures Press, LLC.

Honeycomb Adventure Books are designed with crayon-colored Bible quilts in mind. Trace the square illustrations onto white cotton quilt blocks and color them with Crayola™ crayons. Then press the fabric between paper towels with a hot iron to remove excess wax and make the color permanent. (See more complete instructions at www.biblequilts.com)

Permission is granted to trace or scan the illustrations in this book for use in your family's Bible quilt project or to make a quilt for your church. A PDF file containing each of these pictures is also available to purchasers of this book at

https://honeycombadventures.com/wp-content/uploads/2022/01/Jonah-The-Fearful-Prophet-Bible-quilt-coloring-pages.pdf

www.biblequilts.com   www.honeycombadventures.com

About the author:
Janice D. Green retired as an elementary librarian to write books. She has previously written and published two Bible story books, *The Creation*, and *The First Christmas*. Her passion is to encourage people to read the Bible for themselves and to know that it is true.

About the illustrator:
Kimberly Merritt has been a pastor's wife for over 20 years. While serving beside her husband, she has been blessed to have illustrated over 50 children's books for authors all over the world.

New Releases by Honeycomb Adventures Press, LLC

The latest Honeycomb Adventures books are available in three formats to fit your situation. The full-color edition has always been the standard and continues to be available. E-books and coloring books offer a more economical way to enjoy the stories and illustrations. E-books in full color are the most economical. Coloring books contain everything that is in the full-color format, but also allows the child or an older relative or friend to color the pages and to add his or her name to the cover and title page. All three formats include a link to the downloadable PDF file that contains all the coloring pages and puzzles in the book and information on how to use the coloring pages to make a Bible quilt.

Full Color Picture Books

Full Color E-books

Coloring Books with line drawings

Jonah: The Fearful Prophet shares Jonah's resistance to God's call and his second chance after being rescued from the bottom of the sea by a huge fish. This story also illustrates God's patience with Jonah and with the people of Nineveh.

The Creation gives the day-to-day Genesis account of creation and includes engaging questions for each day to encourage dialogue between the child and caregiver. Also included is a note to encourage parents and youth concerning challenges by the secular world against the creation account.

www.ingramcontent.com/pod-product-compliance
Lightning Source LLC
Chambersburg PA
CBHW060531010526

44110CB00052B/2563